PAUL

By Dan Larsen

*Illustrated by
Al Bohl*

A BARBOUR BOOK

CONTENTS

Trial of Stephen

1
Stephen and Saul

It was winter, and a trial was being held in the Hall of Polished Stones. A man with bound wrists stood in the middle of the court, while the seventy-one judges of the council sat in silence on the great stone benches that curved around the court. Their beards hung to their chests, some to their waists. Their faces were stony. Only their eyes showed their wonder as they listened to the prisoner, Stephen, speak his defense. The charge against him was blasphemy. If they found him guilty he would die.

Stephen was a leader among a group of people in Jerusalem who claimed that a man from Nazareth named Jesus was the long-awaited Messiah. Two years before Jesus had been crucified; but he had risen to life, his followers said, and ruled with God the Father in heaven.

The Messiah had traveled throughout Judea with twelve men he called disciples. At his death these disciples had gone into hiding. But soon they emerged again, speaking boldly of Jesus' resurrection and telling people to believe in Him.

One of the disciples was a man named Peter. In the two years since Jesus' death, Peter had become almost a legend in Jerusalem. He had gone around to the synagogues, preaching about Jesus, the Son of God. He had performed the same miracles that Jesus had. In Jesus' name he had healed the sick, cast out demons, even raised the dead. After hearing Peter, many Jews throughout the city believed in Jesus and formed a group they called "the Way."

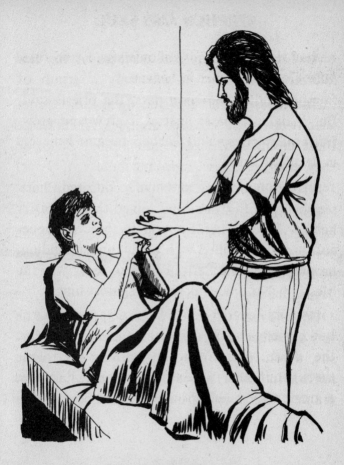

Peter healing the sick

STEPHEN AND SAUL

At first the priests and teachers of the law tolerated the Way. It was only a group of fanatics and would soon pass, the priests said. But it did not pass; instead it grew and grew. Even many priests and teachers became believers in Jesus Christ.

Stephen, a brilliant and highly educated Pharisee, believed in Christ and joined the Way after hearing Peter. Then he went to the synagogues and preached. Filled with a new understanding, he proved by the Scriptures that Jesus was the Messiah. No one could argue against him.

But one man tried. His name was Saul, and he was a teacher in Jerusalem. He came from Tarsus, a center of trade and learning far to the north. His father, a wealthy merchant, had been granted Roman citizenship. Saul had been sent to

Saul of Tarsus

Jerusalem at the age of about thirteen to study the Jewish law and the Holy Scriptures. A gifted student, he became a teacher and lawyer in his early twenties.

Saul only desired to please God and he had believed that strict obedience to the Jewish laws was the way to do so. His love for the law was fierce. He would lay down his life for it.

Then Stephen came along, saying that people could please God not by obeying the law, but simply by believing in his Son, Jesus Christ, the carpenter from Nazareth who had been crucified. "If a man believes in Jesus Christ," Stephen claimed, "then God will consider him righteous." When he heard this, Saul became enraged and decided that Stephen and the Way had to be destroyed.

Saul studying the Holy Scriptures

So Saul challenged Stephen to a public debate. This was the honored Jewish method of settling religious disputes. With the synagogue benches filled, Saul argued that because Jesus had been nailed to a cross, he must have been under God's curse, as it is written in the law.

"But what about the empty tomb?" came the question.

"Jesus' disciples stole the body," Saul answered.

Many people in the audience mumbled. They were not satisfied.

Then Stephen began. He quoted many Scriptures, showing how Moses and the prophets and David and the Psalms all spoke of the coming Messiah. These Scriptures said the Messiah would not come as a conqueror, but would allow

Public debate

himself to be mocked and spit on and murdered, only to rise again and rule forever. Stephen also told about many of the eyewitnesses of Jesus' resurrection. For six weeks after his death, He had appeared to as many as five hundred people, who among many others, were his sworn followers in Jerusalem.

When Stephen finished, the halls resounded with cheers. His argument had clearly won the favor of the people. Many of them became believers.

But Saul became even more determined to stop Stephen. If he could not do it openly, he would do it secretly. He began paying men to go to the council and tell lies about Stephen. These men said Stephen spoke against the law, even against God himself. So the priests had had Stephen

Paying men to lie

arrested and brought before the council.

The accusations were read. Then Stephen was given a chance to defend himself. He began by telling the story, so familiar to the council members, of God's people, Israel. As he talked of Abraham, Jacob, Joseph, and Moses, the men of the council listened as if in a trance. Stephen spoke with power and authority. His face shone like an angel's.

But suddenly Stephen's tone changed. He looked straight at the council. "How stubborn you are!" he said. "How hard are your hearts! How deaf are your ears! You are just like your ancestors. You, too, have resisted the Holy Spirit. Your ancestors killed God's prophets, who long ago announced the coming of His Son. Then *you* murdered His Son! You are the ones

Stephen defending himself

who received God's law, which was handed down by angels. Yet you have not obeyed it!"

Now the members of the council cursed Stephen, their fists knotted, their faces flushed. But he did not notice. He was staring upward, as if right through the ceiling, into heaven.

"Look!" he cried. "I see heaven opened and the Son of Man standing at the right side of God!"

The council members screamed in rage. They rushed to Stephen and dragged him out of the hall, down the steps, into the Court of the Priests, and out into the city street.

They took him out of the northern gate of the city to a place called the Rock of Execution, where the younger men picked up jagged stones and hurled them at Stephen. Soon he fell to his

Stoning Stephen

knees, blood streaming from deep wounds. The stones kept flying.

Saul stood by, the cloaks of the stoners at his feet. A slight smile played on his face. *Now I have beaten you, my enemy!* he thought.

Stephen sagged, his face touching the ground. Through his pain he groaned, "Lord Jesus, do not hold this sin against them!"

The smile froze on Saul's face. He stumbled backward and turned from the scene before him. Suddenly he felt sick. This man was dying, struck down by hateful hands. Yet he responded with love! He did not cry out in pain or rage. Rather, he prayed for his enemies! Saul turned and reeled through the streets like a drunken man. He struggled to understand. How could a man love so much that he forgave his murderers?

Stephen praying for murderers

Saul gritted his teeth against the idea. He told himself, over and over, that a love like that was not possible.

Then began a nightmare for believers in Jerusalem. Saul was given the charge of destroying this new religion. Before Stephen's death, Jesus' followers had enjoyed a limited freedom to worship as they chose. But now they were hunted like animals. Saul went with the temple soldiers into every corner of the city and dragged them into the court to stand trial as Stephen had done.

These followers of Jesus were all brought to the court. There they stood before Saul, who ordered them to curse the name of Jesus. If they refused, they were whipped in public. Men and women alike were tortured like this. A few died from the brutal beatings.

Public beating

STEPHEN AND SAUL

Soon reports came to Saul that some people had escaped to other cities and were preaching about Jesus there. Many had gone to Damascus, to the north of Jerusalem.

Saul's heart grew colder. His purpose was firm. He would pursue the followers of the Way to the ends of the earth, if he had to. He went to the chief priest in Jerusalem and asked for a letter to the Jewish leaders in Damascus. The letter would explain Saul's purpose. Then, Saul knew, the Damascus Jews would be eagerly awaiting his arrival.

Permission to persecute

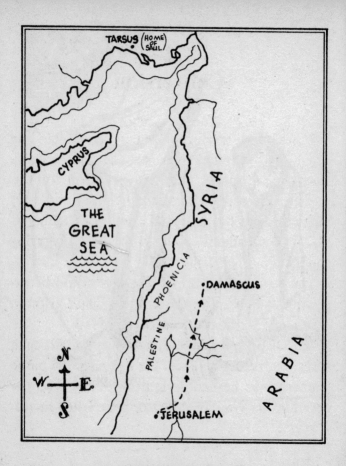

Map of Israel

2
Conversion

It was early spring. The mud of winter had dried, and travelers were on the roads again. Early one morning, Saul left Jerusalem for Damascus. He rode a horse the hundred and sixty miles through the stony hill country of Samaria. A few attendants rode with him, carrying supplies.

The Jewish leaders in Damascus would be expecting Saul. By now the letter the chief priest in Jerusalem had sent would have arrived.

As Saul drew near Damascus, a smile began spreading across his face. He was eager to purge Damascus as he had Jerusalem. Those who believed in the Way must be stopped. When he rid

Damascus of them, he would travel on throughout Palestine until he could wipe out all the followers of Jesus.

About midday the travelers could see the city gates of Damascus. The sky was clear. There was no wind. Suddenly a blinding light burst from the sky just in front of the group. It was far brighter than the sun. The horses reared in terror, throwing their riders to the ground. Saul struggled to his hands and knees. The light was so bright that he held his eyes shut tight.

Just then a great voice came from out of the sky, "Saul, Saul, why do you persecute me?"

Saul opened his eyes. Trembling, he looked up. There before him stood a man of about his own age. Light seemed to flow from him as from a lamp. His robe was so white that Saul had to

A blinding light

shield his eyes. "Who are you, Lord?" asked Saul.

"I am Jesus, whom you are persecuting. It goes hard for you, Saul. You fight against me and against your conscience."

Saul was shaking. "What shall I do, Lord?" he asked.

"Get up and go into Damascus," said Jesus. "There you will be told what to do."

Saul stood up. Jesus was gone. But now Saul could see nothing. Stumbling about, he called to his attendants. "Did you see the Lord?" he asked. "Did you hear him speak?"

"We saw a great light all around us," one said. "But we heard no voice."

"Please," said Saul, "take my hand and lead

"I am Jesus"

me into the city. The Lord told me to go there and wait for him."

The attendants looked at one another in awe. They knew the story of how God had appeared to Moses in the burning bush. Just now they had seen the white light. Could God have appeared to Saul as he had to Moses? Silently, they led Saul into the city.

They guided him down a broad street called Straight to the house of a man named Judas. This man expected Saul, because the Jewish leaders had arranged for Saul to stay here. But Saul asked immediately to be taken upstairs to the guest room and be left alone.

Outside, the sun shone in a blue sky. But Saul lay in darkness. Sounds rose from the street below his window — peddlers crying their wares,

House of Judas

the murmur of voices from passing crowds, and the clop-clop of camels' and donkeys' hooves on the cobblestones. But Saul could hear none of this. In his ears still rang the words of Jesus: *Saul, why do you persecute me?* Now faces flitted past him in his darkness. He saw those Christians he had dragged out of the synagogues and had whipped. *Saul, why do you persecute me?* He saw Stephen, bravely facing the council and bravely dying under their hail of stones. *Saul, why do you persecute me?* He heard Stephen again as he said, "Lord Jesus, do not hold this sin against them." Saul remembered how those words had struck him. They were not spoken in hate, in fear, in vengeance. They were spoken in love. In love! The man's love was stronger even than death, yet Saul had rejected this love. *It*

Alone with his thoughts

goes hard for you, Saul, Jesus said. *You fight against me and against your conscience.*

On the road to Damascus the vision of Stephen praying for his murderers had haunted Saul. But he had gritted his teeth against the vision, more determined than ever not to stop until the last Christian on earth had been destroyed. *You fight against me and against your conscience!*

Saul sat up in a cold sweat. He was shaking. He had no doubt now. Stephen was right. All the Christians were right. *Jesus is alive!* Saul remembered the strong face, the broad shoulders, the scars in His hands and feet. And he remembered the love in His face. Saul had made himself the Lord's enemy. He had set out to destroy all those who worshiped the Lord. Yet the Lord Himself had looked at Saul in love! Forgiveness had filled his voice.

"Jesus is alive!"

CONVERSION

Saul knelt at his bed. "Lord," he said, weeping, "I accept Your forgiveness now. I accept Your love. You are the happiness, the peace, the joy I have sought all my life. It is *not* in the law! It is in You. I ask Your forgiveness for all the evil I have done. I am ready to serve You with all my strength, all my heart, for the rest of my life."

As Saul knelt there a peace came over him that he had never felt before. In his room, in his blindness, he could feel the Lord's presence. Though he could not see Him, he knew Jesus was there. Like a baby in his father's strong arms, Saul fell asleep.

When he woke he prayed. He prayed for hours and hours, until he fell asleep again. Three days passed like this. Saul did not eat or drink. He did not know when it was night or day. He could not

Praying

tell how long he slept or how long he prayed. He did not care. He was in the Lord's presence.

On the morning of the fourth day, Saul's door opened. He heard footsteps. Then he felt a strong hand on his head and heard a man's voice: "Saul, brother, the Lord has sent me to you. In the name of Jesus Christ, receive your sight!"

Suddenly something like scales fell from Saul's eyes. He could see! The morning light flowed through his window. Before him stood a man in a simple robe and a Jewish headdress. "I am Ananias," said the man. "The Lord has sent me to you, and I have obeyed, though at first I was afraid, because I had heard of you. God has chosen you to be a witness for Him to all men, to open their eyes and turn them from darkness to light, from the rule of Satan to God, so that by

"Receive your sight!"

faith in God they may have forgiveness of sins and a place with those whom God has made His own."

Saul just sat there, staring at the man. He was speechless.

"What do you wait for?" said Ananias. "Get up and be baptized so that your sins will be washed away and you will be filled with the Holy Spirit."

Saul was weak from three days with no food or water. Ananias helped him down the stairs and out into a garden behind the house. Here Ananias baptized Saul in a pool of water.

That day the sun had never seemed so bright to Saul, nor the sky so blue. As he walked through the city, he looked at each face with a new interest, a new love.

Baptizing Saul

CONVERSION

That night Ananias brought Saul down a narrow street to a large house where a group of followers of the Way met to worship. Ananias introduced Saul to them. On hearing his name, they gasped.

"Why have you brought him, Ananias?" a man asked. "This man is here to destroy us!"

"Peace, all of you," said Ananias. "The Lord told me in a vision to go to this man, Saul, and baptize him as a believer. He has seen the Lord, on the road here. He believes!"

They stared at Saul for a moment as if they were seeing a ghost. Then one by one they came up to him, embraced him, and gave him the kiss of peace, which in a Jewish home means "welcome, brother."

"This man is here to destroy us!"

CONVERSION

With his new friends, Saul wept and sang praises to God.

That Sabbath Saul went into the synagogue. He wore his Pharisee's blue-fringed robe and turban. By this he was recognized as a teacher, so he was handed the Scripture to read. He read it perfectly, every word, every tone correct, just as he had been taught by the masters in Jerusalem. The leaders of the synagogue nodded in approval as Saul read.

When he had finished, he looked around at the faces in the synagogue. "Friends," he said, "I am here today to proclaim that Jesus Christ is the Son of God."

The people and the leaders were stunned.

Saul told of his seeing Jesus on the road and of the message Ananias had given Saul from God.

Preaching in the synagogue

CONVERSION

But as he spoke, the priests' faces grew flushed with anger. One of them stood up and shook his finger at Saul. "You were sent by the chief priest himself to destroy the work of the Way," he said. "And now you take these people's side! This is betrayal!"

All the other priests began shouting in agreement.

Saul held up his hands. "My brothers," he said, "I have not betrayed God or our religion. I have simply seen the truth. It is my duty to speak the truth I have seen. I did not see a vision, my brothers. Jesus Himself stood in the road before me. I could have touched His hands, His robe, His face. He was killed, as you know. But now He lives. I myself know this because I have seen Him."

"This is betrayal!"

CONVERSION

But the priests would not believe, and the rest of the people in the synagogue rejected him. Under their insults and curses, Saul left the synagogue.

Now he was alone in the city. The Jewish leaders would not listen to him. Other than Ananias's group, the believers in Christ would not accept him, either. The memories of whippings, imprisonment, and death of their fellow believers were too fresh and painful for most of Jesus' followers.

So Saul soon left. He joined a small trading caravan going east. Somewhere in the Arabian Desert, Saul left the caravan and went to live in a cave. He needed time alone. He had brought his scrolls of Scriptures and spent long hours reading them. He prayed and thought. In the day he

Saul leaving Damascus

hunted for food and studied the Scriptures. At night he sat by his cave and stared into the night, thinking. He listened to the desert jackals and hyenas off in the darkness. Sometimes the roar of a lion would break the stillness of the night. Saul's flickering camp fire kept them from coming too close.

Every now and then caravans of traders from the east passed near Saul's cave. He would welcome the travelers to his cave and give them shelter and food. Many of them became believers in Christ after listening to Saul tell of his faith.

Three years passed. Saul was burned dark by the sun. He was lean and sinewy. Now, with a new power, he could prove by Scriptures that Jesus is the Messiah and Son of God. He was ready to begin his work.

Desert cave

CONVERSION

First Saul returned to Damascus. There he spoke with a new boldness. He recited Scriptures, showing how all the prophecies of the Messiah fit Jesus. Many Jews believed, but not the priests. Since they could not argue against Saul, and they could not defeat him in public, they began plotting to kill him.

Soon a band of cutthroats, hired by the priests, stole through the city looking for Saul, waiting for their chance. A dark alley, a thrust of the knife, and they would be paid handsomely. Another group waited just outside the city gates, in case Saul tried to leave that way.

Saul's friends who believed in Jesus learned of this plot. They hid him during the day. One night they lowered him down the city wall in a fish basket. He vanished into the desert night.

Narrow Escape

Seeking friends

3
The Hidden Years

Saul went to Jerusalem. This time, though, he did not go into the synagogue. Instead he sought out believers in Christ. These were his only friends now. His fellow Pharisees no longer accepted him.

But even the followers of the Way were wary of him. It had been more than three years since Saul had left Jerusalem for Damascus, but the painful memories of his persecution of believers were still fresh. Jesus' followers lived in hiding now and worshiped secretly. They feared Saul too much to believe he had seen Jesus and become a believer.

So Saul was alone. He wandered the streets at

night, wondering what would happen next. He had no friends in Jerusalem, only Jewish enemies who hated him and followers of Jesus who feared him. It was a bitter time.

But one man believed Saul. He came up to him in the street one night. "I am Barnabas," he said. "I have heard the story of your conversion, brother Saul. Come with me. I will take you to a place where you can stay."

Barnabas led Saul through the dark streets to a small house and knocked on the door.

"Who comes at this hour?" came a voice from inside.

"Barnabas. I come in the name of the Lord, and I bring a brother in the faith."

The door opened. There stood a man of about Saul's age, thirty-five. A thick, black beard

"I am Barnabas"

bushed out over his broad chest. He wore a coarse, short tunic and sandals. His arms and legs were knotted with muscle. Across his bare shoulders were ribbonlike scars. He looked strong enough to wrestle a lion. But his face was calm, and his eyes shone with burning brightness.

Saul fought an impulse to kneel before this man. He felt he was in the presence of a king.

"Peter," said Barnabas, "this is Saul, he who used to persecute believers. He has seen Jesus and is now His follower, too."

Saul was afraid now. He expected anger, hatred. But Peter, who knew Saul had been his worst enemy, stepped up to Saul and embraced him warmly. "Welcome to my home, my brother," Peter said.

Peter

For two weeks Saul stayed with Peter, listening to him tell of his travels with Jesus of Nazareth. To a Jew of that day, nothing was more important in his education than memorizing sacred Scriptures and teachings. As Peter shared all the parables and teachings of Jesus with Saul, he recalled everything, down to the last word, even recalling the tone in Jesus' voice as he had spoken.

During these two weeks Saul came to know his Lord much better. As Peter spoke of Jesus his words seemed to come alive and burrow deep into Saul's mind and spirit. Peter and Saul formed a deep friendship that would last for the rest of their lives.

Now Saul burned like a torch. He went to the synagogue and spoke boldly about Jesus. He debated with the priests and teachers, and he

Learning from Peter

proved to everyone who listened that Jesus is the Messiah. Some believed. Others refused. Soon there were rumors of another plot against Saul.

One night, as had happened in Damascus, a group of believers whisked Saul out of the city.

He returned to Tarsus, the place of his birth. The city lay on the northeast corner of the Mediterranean Sea, between the sea and the great snow-capped Taurus Mountains to the north.

Tarsus was a center of pagan religion. Many, many gods were worshiped there. Numerous Jews lived there, too, and they had their synagogues. Here Saul lived like a Jew, obeying their laws and worshiping in their synagogues. But his heart was full of love, and his love was for all men, not Jews only. He spoke to everyone, in every religion, about Jesus Christ.

Escaping a murder plot

The Jewish leaders in Tarsus rejected Saul. They would not listen to his message and ordered him to stop preaching. But he could not stop. He knew the truth, the truth that would set people free, and he had to speak it.

Now Saul himself was whipped, as many who believed in Jesus had been whipped under his orders. In Tarsus he was whipped five times. Each whipping was according to Roman law, which allowed up to, but not more than, thirty-nine lashes. Using all his might, the lictor, the whipping man, lashed down over one shoulder so the cords would reach the chest. He did this thirteen times. Then he gave thirteen lashes on the back, across one shoulder, then thirteen across the other. The pain was like molten lead being poured into open wounds as the whip snapped

Thirty-nine Lashes

again and again into cuts it had already opened.

After each whipping, Saul was carried to his father's house to recover. Before he left Tarsus, he was scarred for life. Though he was not tall, he had been strongly built from years of training in gymnastics, but now, although he was barely forty years old, he was bowlegged and slightly stooped. His brow was creased as if he walked in constant pain. This was the look, common for slaves taken in war, of a man who had been severely beaten.

The Jews cast him out of the synagogues. His own family cast him out of his home. He was alone again, but now he wore the marks of his faith in Jesus — the ugly, jagged scars on his back and chest. He disappeared into the foothills of the Taurus Mountains.

Leaving Tarsus

THE HIDDEN YEARS

Saul was a wounded man. He had been strong and fearless. Now his body and his will were broken. He went slowly up into the hills and found a deep, dry cave. There he prayed for strength and courage. *Was it all for nothing?* he wondered.

But God answered his prayer. One night Saul had a vision. He felt himself taken up, up, through the clouds into heaven. He was shown what he later called "the third heaven." The vision was so beautiful it would sustain him in the coming years of endless travel and hardships. But Saul was told not to tell what he saw. The vision was for him alone. It was God's gift to Saul, and it helped him find new faith. He would later write, "The sufferings of this present time are not worthy to be compared with the glory that

Saul taken into heaven

shall be revealed."

The Jewish leaders had rejected Saul's message. So he went now to the farms and small villages in the Taurus Mountains, telling people about Jesus. Many people listened to him and believed. As he traveled here he thought often of the parable Jesus had told about the rich man who prepared a feast for his friends. None of them would come, so the man went out into the streets and called in the poor, the sick, the blind, and the lame. *Your people, the Jews, will not hear my message, Lord,* thought Saul. *May I not invite to your feast the other peoples of the world?*

During this time Saul also sailed along the coast, visiting the towns of the northern Mediterranean. He would later write that he was shipwrecked twice during this time. Once he drifted

Sailing the Mediterranean

on the open sea "for a day and a night."

Eight years after Saul fled Jerusalem, he was still traveling alone, visiting and revisiting many farms and villages. In one of the villages Barnabas found him.

"I have been searching many months for you," Barnabas said. "My brother, I have not forgotten you. Nor has your brother Peter. I live now in the city of Antioch in Syria. There is a growing church of believers there. Many, many Jews there now follow Christ, and those who believe are called Christians. This church needs strong leaders. Though I am doing what I can, I am only one man. I need help. Will you come to Antioch with me?"

Saul stared for a moment. Then he stammered, "My brother, I am only the Lord's hum-

"I have been searching for you."

ble servant. If it is His will, then I will go with you and help in any way I can."

So Saul set out for Antioch with Barnabas. They traveled by land along the coast around the northeasternmost point of the Mediterranean, then south. In Antioch Saul was received in love and warmth. For the first time in many years he had a home.

In the year 46 A.D. there was a famine in Judea, which a prophet in the church of Antioch had foretold a few years earlier. The leaders there had believed him and had sent out Christians all over the land to buy and store corn. Now the church appointed Saul and Barnabas to take some corn to the people in Jerusalem. They took a young Greek Christian named Titus with them.

In Jerusalem Saul and Barnabas gave the corn

Taking corn to Jerusalem

to the leaders of the Christian church. The leaders in turn distributed it to the people in the city, both Christians and Jews.

Saul met with the leaders of the Christians: Peter, James, and John. Saul told them of his sufferings in Tarsus and of the many believers now in the mountains and coastal villages. These believers were not Jews but of many different races.

"I believe the message of the gospel is for all people, not just Jews," said Saul. The leaders agreed. Peter, too, believed that God meant all people to be saved. The leaders then appointed Saul and Barnabas to go throughout the world and bring the message to everyone.

Saul decided he would begin in Jerusalem. He would return to the synagogue, where ten years

"The gospel is for all people"

ago he had been rejected. *This time they will listen!* he thought.

But one night he heard the voice of the Lord. "Leave Jerusalem quickly, for they will not accept your testimony about me here! Go! For I am sending you far away, to the Gentiles."

Hearing the voice of the Lord

Laying hands on Saul

4
The First Mission

Barnabas and Saul first returned to Antioch in Syria, where the leaders of the church laid hands on them and blessed them for their upcoming mission. It was decided that John Mark, the nephew of Barnabas, would go with the two.

They set sail for the island of Cyprus, about a hundred miles west and south of Antioch. After a visit to the port of Salamis, they sailed around the southern coast of the island, stopping at each of the small towns along the coast and preaching in the synagogues. Finally they came to the city of Paphos on the west coast of the island.

For several days they preached in the synagogue there. Then one day a summons came from the Roman proconsul of Cyprus, Sergius Paulus, who wished to hear Saul speak. So Saul, Barnabas, and John Mark set out at once for the palace.

The palace sat on a hill overlooking the city. As the three men approached the great stone gates, the guards on top of the wall saluted them. The gates swung open, and a man came out and bowed. "Welcome, honored guests of the proconsul," he said.

Inside, the proconsul greeted the men from his throne. The hall had no walls, only tall pillars on either side that supported a great arched roof. From his throne the proconsul could look out over the bleached-white buildings of the city to the dark-blue water of the silent bay.

"Come forward, guests," he said. "I have

Welcome, honored guests

heard of your preaching in the synagogue here. I am curious to hear of this Jesus you speak of. Please tell me of him.''

Barnabas motioned for Saul to speak. So Saul began with Scriptures that foretold the Messiah's coming and told how He would suffer and die and then rise to life. He gave example after example that testified or verified that Jesus is the Messiah. The proconsul's face grew intent as he listened to Saul. He had never heard of anything so strange, so wonderful as this. Never had he encountered anyone like Saul, who spoke so clearly and so convincingly.

But as Saul spoke, he noticed a man at the proconsul's side and recognized him as a Jew named Bar-Jesus who called himself Elymas, which means ''skillful'' or ''sage.'' This Elymas, the

Elymas

proconsul's advisor called himself a holy prophet and a "wise man of the East." Saul knew him as an evil man who dabbled in sorcery.

Suddenly Elymas shouted, "Do not listen to this, my lord Paulus! This man speaks lies! He is trying to infect you with these lies. This Jesus of whom he speaks is dead. He was executed under our holy law because he claimed to be the Son of God."

The proconsul looked startled.

Elymas pointed at Saul and his two companions. "These men are not true to their own religion," Elymas continued. "They have —"

"Silence!" said Saul. The sorcerer's face flushed with rage. Saul pointed at him and said, "You son of the devil! You enemy of all goodness, full of all lies and wicked cunning! Is it not

"Silence!"

time you stopped making crooked the ways of the Lord?"

A fire burned in Saul's eyes. He seemed to grow taller. All eyes in the hall were on him. Elymas seemed to shrink before him.

"Look now!" said Saul. "The hand of the Lord strikes you! You will be blind, and for a time you shall not see the light!"

Elymas shrieked and stumbled forward with his arms outstretched. "I cannot see!" he cried. "Help me!"

Just as Saul in his blindness had once been led, Elymas was now led by the hand out of the great hall.

The proconsul came up to Saul. He was pale and shaking. He fell on his knees. "I believe that Jesus is the Messiah and Lord!" he said. "Please

"I cannot see!"

baptize me now. I wish to follow him, too!"

Later, when the three travelers sailed from Cyprus, they rejoiced. A Roman official was now a Christian. Saul adopted the name *Paul,* the Roman version of his name. From here on he would be known to Christians throughout the world as the Apostle Paul.

The men sailed north and landed in the port of Attalia. From there it was a short walk north to Perga. Paul wanted to continue north over the Taurus Mountains and then through the vast tracts of raw wilderness to the great city of Antioch in Pisidia.

John Mark turned back at Perga. Whether he feared the mountains ahead or just felt homesick, he did not say. But he returned the way they had come. Paul and Barnabas joined a trading

Walking to Perga

caravan and went on.

The ancient Roman road here went straight up without switchbacks. The climb was very steep, and the going was painfully slow. As the road climbed, the slopes grew barren. Near the top, gnarled pine trees wrestled with giant boulders.

Once Paul and Barnabas reached the top of the mountains, travel became even more difficult. Narrow, swinging footbridges spanned great chasms of ice and snow, with wild, rushing rivers far below.

Rome's strong arm of protection did not reach this far. Robbers and murderers lived in these mountains. Fierce, wild barbarians preyed on anyone who dared travel alone or in small parties.

The men of the caravan kept a fire going

Perilous journey

throughout the bitter nights and slept huddled around the flames. Every night a sentry, wrapped in thick woolen blankets, kept careful watch.

After many days they passed out of the peaks and went down into more friendly highlands, the region of Galatia. Here the caravan split up, and Paul and Barnabas went on alone.

For three days they walked on a path by a lake called Limnai. Ahead loomed the great snow-capped Mount Olympus. At night the two men found lodging at one of the few cottages in the area.

Finally they came to Pisidian Antioch. Paul preached in the synagogue, and the Jews listened in wonder. Many of them became believers. Paul and Barnabas stayed here through the summer,

Keeping careful watch

building up the number of believers among both Jews and Greeks.

But the unbelieving Jews slowly began to organize a plot against the two men. The priests went throughout the city telling lies against them. These stories reached the ears of the city officials. One day Paul and Barnabas were arrested and whipped with the thirty-nine lashes. Then they were dragged out of the city and ordered never to return.

The two men rested for a few days at the house of one of the Christian families of Antioch. With their wounds barely healed, they set out east and south for the ancient city of Iconium.

In Iconium, as in the synagogues in other cities, Paul wore his Pharisee's robe and turban so the synagogue leaders would recognize him as a

Dragging Paul from the city

scholar and an authority and ask him to read the Scriptures and preach. When Paul spoke about Jesus, faces in the gatherings showed astonishment. In Iconium hundreds of Jews and Greeks became believers.

But Iconium, too, eventually rejected the good news. When the unbelieving Jews had stirred up enough anger and hatred among the people, they could then have Paul and Barnabas arrested, whipped or stoned, and thrown out of the city.

It went like this in Antioch, Iconium, and Lystra in the Galatian region. Of these times Paul would later write: "For His sake I suffered the loss of everything, but I consider it useless garbage compared with being able to win Christ."

But even as they lay recovering from their painful beatings, Paul and Barnabas rejoiced.

Stoning Paul

"You will be hated for My name's sake," Jesus had told His apostles. And always the Lord gave them strength to endure. "I have the strength to face all conditions, by the power that Christ gives me," Paul would write.

When Paul left Lystra, he was bruised and battered from a stoning. He and Barnabas traveled east and south to Derbe, where they stayed through the winter while Paul healed. The two men made many disciples that winter. These Christians loved and took care of them.

In the spring the men returned the way they had come. In each city they found many of the Christians they had converted and stayed with them for a little while, praying with them and encouraging them to keep on in faith.

Paul writing

Sharing with believers

5
The Second Mission

On a summer day in Antioch of Syria the Christians went around from house to house, telling the good news — Paul and Barnabas were back.

The next night the Christians gathered in a large open-air atrium, on the roof of a house on Singon Street. Each believer listened eagerly as Paul and Barnabas told of their travels and marveled at the voyages over the sea, a thousand miles of travel on foot, and the ice-covered Taurus Mountains. How thrilling to hear of the miracles God had performed and of the many, many new Christians!

The two men did not tell of the whippings and

stonings. But their listeners knew. They could see the fresh scars on neck and shoulder and face. They could see the added lines of pain in Paul's face, the greater stoop to his shoulders, the slower pace of his walk.

Yet even more light shone in Paul's eyes, even more power echoed in his voice. With increased suffering came increased faith.

Paul and Barnabas stayed in Antioch several months. They resumed their roles of preaching and teaching. This was a good time to rest, to let old wounds heal, to gain strength.

As the months passed, though, Paul grew restless. He wanted to travel again, to spread the news of Jesus Christ throughout the world. The words of the Lord came to him now, over and over: "Go! For I am sending you far away to the

Paul growing restless

Gentiles.''

Then news came that made Paul more eager than ever to leave. In the Galatian cities Paul and Barnabas had visited new converts had begun to turn from the faith. A group of Pharisees from Jerusalem traveled through Galatia, telling the new Christians that the Jewish law was the only way to salvation. On hearing this, many believers lost faith.

Paul was angry. He loved every believer as his own child and could not bear the thought of any turning away from Christ. God had given man the law as a way to prove that man could not be righteous by his own strength; Paul had known that was true of himself. He had known the whole law yet had not been able to obey it all. Only by the power Jesus Christ gave him could

Receiving bad news

he live free of sin. Later, in a letter to Christians in Rome, he wrote, "We know that the law is spiritual, but I am a mortal man, sold as a slave to sin. I do not understand what I do, for I do not do what I want to do, but instead I do what I hate.... My inner being delights in the law of God. But I see a different law at work in my body — a law that fights against the law my mind approves of. It makes me a prisoner to the law of sin that is at work in my body.... Who will rescue me from this body that is taking me to death? Thanks be to God, who does this through our Lord Jesus Christ!"

Paul knew this was the truth. But now people in Galatia were being lied to. Those believing this lie would turn from life to death!

Paul felt an agony in his soul. He decided he must write a letter. Quickly he called for a pen-

Christians being lied to

man. He wanted to dictate, not write. This way he could think faster, and his words would sound more like his own speech, as if he were right there with the Galatians as they read his letter. With the penman scribbling furiously, Paul spoke to the Galatians.

"I am astonished," he said. "You are so quickly deserting the one who called you by the grace of Christ and are accepting another gospel — not that there is another gospel, but there are some who trouble you and want to pervert the gospel of Christ. If anyone should preach to you a gospel different from the one we preached to you, may he be condemned to hell!

"Let me tell you, my brothers, that the gospel I preach did not come from any man. Jesus Christ himself revealed it to me. What I write is

Dictating the Galatian letter

true. God knows that I am not lying! A person is put right with God only through faith in Jesus Christ, never by doing what the law requires. If a person is put right with God through the law, it means that Christ died for nothing!

"You foolish Galatians! Who put a spell on you? You were given a clear description of the death of Jesus Christ on the cross. Tell me, did you receive God's Spirit by doing what the law requires or by hearing the gospel and believing it? How can you be so foolish? You began by God's Spirit. Do you now want to finish by your own power?

"The law came simply to show us the power of sin in man. Christ came to set us free from the power of sin. So let his Spirit direct your lives, and you will not satisfy the evil desires of human

"You foolish Galatians!"

nature. What human nature does is quite plain. It shows itself in immoral, filthy, and indecent actions. People become enemies, and they fight. They become jealous, angry, and ambitious. They are envious, get drunk, have orgies, and do other things like these. I warn you now as I have before: those who do these things will not possess the kingdom of God.

"But the Spirit produces love, joy, peace, patience, kindness, goodness, faithfulness, humility, and self-control. Those who belong to Jesus Christ have put to death their human nature with all its passions and desires.

"As for those who follow this rule in their lives, may peace and mercy be with them. May the grace of our dear Lord Jesus Christ be with you all, my brothers. Amen."

Fruit of the Spirit

THE SECOND MISSION

Paul had this letter copied and stamped with the seal of the Christian church in Antioch. Then he sent it to the Christians in Galatia. He stayed on in Antioch, busy with his work in the church. But his heart yearned to visit his "children" in all the cities he and Barnabas had gone to.

Finally, almost two years later, the time came. It was spring in the year 50 A.D. Paul was about fifty years old as he set out north again. He went by land this time, going around the northeastern point of the Mediterranean Sea, then heading west for Derbe. At Derbe, Silas, another Christian, joined him. They continued west through Iconium, Lystra, Antioch in Pisidia, on to the coastal city of Troas. As they traveled, Paul learned to his joy that the Galatian Christians had heeded his letter.

Traveling again

THE SECOND MISSION

From Troas the men sailed north and west to the city of Philippi. In this bustling military center the streets teemed with Roman soldiers — brawny young men and grizzled old veterans. Paul and Silas's first convert here was a woman named Lydia, who sold expensive purple-dyed cloth. After Paul spoke to her about Jesus, he baptized her in the little Gangites River, just outside the city. Now full of joy and the love of God, she invited the men to stay at her house. Here they had food and shelter and fellowship while in Philippi. Lydia's family and servants all became believers, too.

But trouble came quickly. Daily the men went to the river to pray. A girl started following them, crying out, "These men are servants of the Supreme God and are telling of the way to salva-

Baptizing Lydia

tion!'' She kept this up for about four days. At first Paul tolerated her, though she was a nuisance to them. But then he began to feel uneasy about her. There was something eerie in her voice, something strange in her face. Then the Spirit of God showed him the truth: *She was demon-possessed!*

On seeing this, Paul turned to her. Though he pointed at her, the words he spoke were not to her. "I command you in the name of Jesus Christ to come out of her!" he said.

At once the wild look left her face. Her shoulders dropped. She sighed as if in relief.

Many in the small crowd around them gasped in astonishment. Some drew back from Paul as if he were a god.

A group of richly dressed men hustled out of

The demon possessed girl

the crowd and formed a knot together.

"See what this man has done!" one of them hissed. "He has cast the spirit of prophecy from this slave girl of ours! Look at her! She is in her right mind now."

"And will no longer be able to prophesy for us," said another.

"Listen," said the first. "We have made a fortune with her. Now all is lost. We must destroy these two men. They have been preaching about some new god. Let us bring charges against them and have them thrown into prison. Then perhaps we can find another prophet."

The men rushed at Paul and Silas, grabbed them, and dragged them to the city magistrates.

"These men are causing a disturbance in our city!" one of the group said. "They are Jews, in

Dragging them to the city leaders

the first place."

That was bad. To the magistrates, Jews were troublemakers. Claudius, the Roman emperor, had recently forced the Jewish people to leave Rome.

"And they speak against Roman authority!" lied another.

A crowd gathered. There were many angry faces, many shouts and threats. The magistrates had to do something.

Strong men dragged Paul and Silas to flogging posts in the street, and tore their cloaks from their backs, tied the two Christians to the posts and beat them with wooden rods. As wounds — old and new — opened and blood spurted from their backs, the crowd roared.

Another flogging

Then the two men were dragged down the street to the prison, cut into a steep hillside. Their ankles were locked together with wooden stocks, and they were thrown into a dank, dark cave inside the prison. A heavy barred door clanged shut.

Paul and Silas were bleeding, cold, and aching. Because their raw backs stung so much, they could not sit against the rough stone wall. Their feet were in such agony in the stocks that they could not stand up. They sat in water that trickled from the walls and in blood that trickled from their backs. Both began to pray.

Soon their prayers became praises, and their praises became songs that filled the dark, stuffy dungeon and reached out into every cell, where other prisoners sat silently, listening and

Paul and Silas in Prison

wondering.

Sometime in the night, as the two voices rang on and on, the ground suddenly shook. The prison bars rattled and suddenly all the prison doors flew open and the stocks on Paul and Silas's ankles burst apart. As suddenly as it had come, the earthquake stopped.

The jailer rushed in, with several servants following. "Quick!" he cried. "Bring a light!"

One servant brought the jailer a torch. With a shaking hand he grasped it and went into the prison. He saw all the cell doors open, some hanging from broken hinges. *An escape!* he thought. A prison escape would mean his execution. He drew his sword and was about to plunge it into his breast when a sharp command stopped him.

"Wait! We are all here." The voice came from

The jailer about to kill himself

the cave that held the two new prisoners. Even more terrified, the jailer thought, *When I brought them in here last night, I knew they were somehow different!* He had heard the story of the possessed girl and Paul. People told him the two men preached about a new god, someone named Jesus, who they said was crucified and rose to life. Now the jailer knew this earthquake was the power of God. He entered the cave and fell on his knees before Paul and Silas.

"Sirs," he said, "what must I do to be saved?"

"Put your trust in the Lord Jesus," Paul answered. "And you will be saved, you and all your household."

The jailer led the two men to his house nearby and washed their wounds in a well. There Paul

"How can I be saved?"

baptized the man and his whole family.

When dawn came the family was sitting around the dining table listening in wonder to Paul as he spoke of Jesus Christ.

Household salvation

Tent making

6
The Third Mission

From Philippi, Paul and Silas journeyed south again, through Thessalonica, Berea, and Athens, to Corinth. In Corinth, Paul stayed for about two years with a Christian man and wife, Aquila and Priscilla. They were tent makers by trade. Paul worked with them while he stayed there, earning his own living.

From Corinth, Paul sailed east across the Aegean Sea to Asia. He landed in Ephesus, a city famous for wizardry and sorcery. Aquila and Priscilla went with Paul and found a home in Ephesus. But Paul went on, sailing west and south across the Mediterranean Sea to Jerusalem. He had been gone several years. On this second journey he had been imprisoned, whipped, beaten, and thrown out of synagogues and cities. Yet the gospel was spreading. The number of Christians in every city grew steadily.

When Paul arrived in Jerusalem, he was nearly sixty. He was almost crippled from his many injuries. But Paul was not ready to rest. He stayed only a few days visiting his friends. Then he set out again.

He went north by land through the cities in Galatia, visiting all the Christian churches there. Next he went west to Ephesus, where he stayed again with Aquila and Priscilla.

Here many Greeks and Jews became believers. Paul spoke in the synagogue on the Sabbath days, until the unbelieving Jews drove him out. When he left, many Jews and Greeks went with

Sharing the good news

him, and they met in one another's homes. Paul stayed in Ephesus through the winter of 52 A.D.

Ephesus became the training center for Christian missionaries to surrounding cities. Christianity spread like fire across the continent. Luke would later write that "all the people who lived in the province of Asia, both Jews and Greeks, heard the Word of the Lord."

Paul longed to visit all the cities to encourage the Christians. But for the moment, too much was happening at Ephesus. The light of the gospel was shining into all the deepest, darkest corners of that city. William Shakespeare, an English playwright and poet, would write centuries later that Ephesus was full of "dark-working sorcerers that change the mind." As Paul taught and preached, many people became believers.

Ephesus

Miracles happened in the church. The sick were healed, and demons were cast out. Christians came forward with their ancient books of sorcery and witchcraft and burned them publicly.

As in every other city where Paul preached, the unbelieving Jews caused him trouble.

When people left the Jewish synagogues, they took their money for tithes and offerings with them. Now they gave to the Christian church. The Jewish treasury was getting low. In the summer of 53 A.D. the Jewish leaders went to Marcus Silanus, the Roman proconsul of Asia, and charged Paul with robbery of the Jewish temple. Silanus had no choice but to arrest Paul.

Paul waited in prison more than a year before Silanus would hear his case. During this time he was allowed to have visitors. Many of his Chris-

Burning sorcery books

tian friends came to see him. Among them were Aquila and Priscilla, Luke, and his two special young friends, Titus and Timothy. Here Paul also wrote letters to Christian churches in Asia and Macedonia.

He was released in the spring of 54 A.D. The Jews could not prove their accusations in court. Paul now had the protection of proconsul Silanus, and he stayed on in Ephesus for several more months.

Then evil struck. Silanus was murdered. His cousin, Nero, had just seized power in Rome by murdering his adopted father, Claudius. To keep his cousin from claiming the throne in Rome, Nero had Silanus murdered, too. Now anyone who had been loyal to Silanus or anyone under his protection, like Paul, was in grave danger.

Nero

THE THIRD MISSION

Danger did not wait long to find Paul. Sometime in early 55 A.D., he was seized and tortured brutally, almost to death, then thrown in prison.

It was a dark, evil time for Paul. Alone, racked with pain, cold, and sick with a burning fever, he began to wonder if his faith would last.

It did. In this time of agony and despair he found the strength in Christ to survive. Paul would later write about this time. "The Lord said to me, 'My grace is sufficient for you, for my strength is made perfect in weakness.' Praise to our God and Father, the God of all comfort, who comforts us in all our affliction.

"I was afflicted," he wrote, "but not crushed, in sorrow but not driven to despair, persecuted but not forsaken, struck down but not destroyed — always being given up to death for Jesus'

Paul ill

sake, so that the life of Jesus may be manifested.''

One thing could never be taken from Paul. ''I am certain,'' he wrote, ''that nothing can separate us from His love. Neither death nor life, neither angels nor other heavenly rulers or powers, neither the present nor the future, neither the world above nor the world below — there is nothing in all creation that will ever be able to separate us from the love of God which is ours through Christ Jesus our Lord.''

So the love of Christ made it possible for him to survive this time. After a year, somehow his friends Priscilla and Aquila gained his release, either by pleading with officials or by raising money from the Christian churches.

Paul felt it was time to leave Ephesus. He went

Being released from jail

north to Troas. Here was a small but active Christian church, believers whom he had baptized on his first visit, years earlier.

That night the Christians were packed into the third-floor room of a house in the heart of the city. It was a cool April night, but in that crowded room, with the oil lamps burning hot, the air grew warm and close. Paul spoke long into the night, teaching all that he knew about the Lord Jesus. The people sat listening in wonder and joy, hungry for every word.

No one noticed a young man sitting on the open window ledge as his head began to nod. No one saw as his head dropped to his chest, and he began to snore.

Paul's voice droned on and on.

Suddenly a woman screamed. "Eutychus! My

Eutychus!

Eutychus! He has fallen from the window!''

Several men rushed to the window. There on the street, three stories below, lay the boy. Now the group began scrambling down the stairs, wailing and praying aloud.

Luke the physician was among the first to reach the boy. He laid his ear to the boy's chest. Then he stood up slowly. "He is dead," he said softly. Now wails and cries broke out louder. The boy's mother collapsed on the still body and sobbed uncontrollably. Several people just stood there in stunned silence, tears streaming down their faces.

Suddenly Paul burst down the stairway. Gently, he pulled the boy's mother aside. Then he knelt down and, like a shepherd tenderly picking up a newborn lamb, he scooped up the boy's

He's dead!

body and held it tightly in his arms. The people drew back in silence.

"Do not weep," Paul said. "He is alive." A sudden shudder shook the boy's body, then a cough. His eyes opened!

Weeping and praising God, the people joyfully carried Eutychus back upstairs. Paul continued speaking through the night.

Early in the morning they shared the bread and wine, as their Lord had shown them. Just before light, Paul said good-bye and left.

Paul was eager to return to Jerusalem, but he had been warned not to go. Recently many prophecies had warned that danger awaited him there. His Christian brothers and sisters begged him to stay away.

So Paul walked alone on the road south to

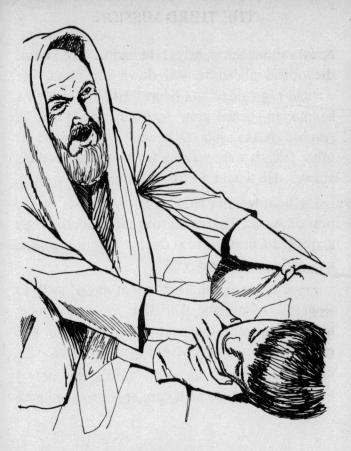

"He is alive"

Assos, about thirty miles. He had sent Luke and the others ahead to sail down the coast. He wanted time alone. As he walked he prayed. As he prayed, peace grew in his heart. When he reached Assos, late that night, Luke and his other friends were waiting for him. Paul had his answer: He would go to Jerusalem.

He boarded the ship with his friends in the port of Assos. That night they sailed south. They arrived at Chios the next day, at Samos the next, and Miletus the next.

From Miletus, Paul sent a messenger north to Ephesus, asking the Christian leaders to meet him. They came the next day. Once they had gathered, Paul stood before them to speak.

"My brothers," he said, "you know how I have spent my time with you, how I worked with

Paul at sea

many tears and humility during the hard times I suffered because of the unbelieving Jews. Now, in obedience to the Holy Spirit, I am going to Jerusalem, not knowing what will happen to me there. I only know the Holy Spirit has warned me that troubles wait for me. But I consider my own life to be nothing. I only want to complete my mission and finish the work the Lord Jesus gave me to do, which is to declare the good news about the grace of God. I know that none of you will ever see me again. So keep watch over yourselves and over all the flock that the Holy Spirit has placed in your care. When I leave, fierce wolves will come among you, and they will not spare the flock. Keep watch, then. Now I leave you in the care of God.''

His friends came to him, embracing him and

Paul sharing his heart

weeping. Some begged him not to go. "You will be in danger!" they reminded him.

"What are you doing, crying like this and breaking my heart?" said Paul, weeping, too. "I am ready to go to prison or even to die for the sake of the Lord Jesus."

All his friends walked slowly with him down to the ship, still weeping. There they said their last farewells.

I am ready to go to Prison

Trying to correct Paul

7
A Prisoner

In Jerusalem the Christian leaders greeted Paul warmly. They listened intently as he reported everything the Lord had done in all the places of his travels. But when he had finished, one leader drew him aside.

"Brother Paul," he said, "many Jews have come to believe in the Lord Jesus. But these people still practice the law and the customs. Stories have gone around here saying that you preach against the law of Moses and against the temple. These Christian Jews would not accept you if they knew you were here now. We, the leaders, feel that if you would go into the temple and commit the purification ritual for four days, these Jews would see that you obey the law yourself, and there would be no trouble because of you."

"It goes against my judgment to behave so falsely," said Paul. "But I would do anything so that no one would lose faith in the Lord, and I will do what you say."

This decision, made in love, would cost Paul his freedom.

Paul did as he had promised. As he stood in an inner room of the temple with four other Jews who were performing the same ritual, suddenly a shout came, "Men of Israel, help! This is the man who preaches to everyone everywhere against our people and our law. Now he has defiled our temple by bringing Greeks here!"

As soon as the speaker opened his mouth Paul

"Men of Israel, help!"

recognized him. He and the others with him were Jews from Asia who had stirred up much trouble against Paul. Before the apostle could answer that the men with him were not Greeks, but Jews, the men at the door grabbed him. They dragged him out of the temple and into the street. Other Jews in the temple had heard the cry. They joined the first group, screaming and shouting. More and more Jews gathered. They dragged Paul, kicking and punching him. In no time he would have been torn to pieces.

Suddenly a clang of steel rang out. Roman soldiers waded through the mob, flinging Jews left and right. They tore Paul's attackers off him and carried him out of the street, up the stairs to the tower of Lysias, the commander. Lysias had seen the uproar and ordered the soldiers to arrest

Riot in the Temple

Paul.

The mob surged around the steps. "Kill him!" they screamed. "He's not fit to live!" The heavy doors of the tower slammed shut.

Inside, Paul slumped to his knees. Two soldiers helped him up. They led Paul down a set of stairs, through a low archway, and into a large room lit with torches along the walls. Lysias mumbled an order to a centurion standing there, then turned and climbed the stairs and went down a hall to his quarters.

The centurion motioned to the soldiers. They tied Paul's wrists with leather thongs, which they threw over a wooden beam overhead. Then they pulled the thongs until his arms were stretched taut over his head. Next they ripped his cloak off his torso.

Paul in Lysias tower

This position meant only one thing, Paul knew. The dreaded flagellum! This was a scourge used to torture criminals before crucifixion or to force a prisoner to talk. The scourge was made with leather lashes into which were tied jagged pieces of bone or steel. Few survived the whipping. Even if they did, nerves, muscles, even organs would be torn to shreds. Paul, with his back already a mass of knotted weals and scars, would not live through it.

The lictor stepped forward. Paul said, "Is it lawful for you to scourge a Roman citizen without a trial?"

Everyone drew back, eyes wide. The centurion dashed up the stairs. In a moment he returned with Lysias.

"Tell me," said Lysias, "are you a Roman

The dreaded Flagellum!

citizen?''

"I am," said Paul. "I was born a free Roman citizen."

"Quickly!" said Lysias. "Cut him down!" Then he himself helped Paul up the stairs and down the hall to his own quarters. It was not legal for a Roman citizen to be punished without a trial. Anyone violating that law would be executed.

Lysias felt afraid. He had nothing to report to his superiors about the cause of this riot today. No one had brought formal charges against this prisoner here. What would he do?

The next day Lysias ordered the Jewish council to meet in their court, the Hall of Polished Stones. He brought Paul to stand before them and offer his defense.

Lysias helping Paul

Paul stood now where about thirty years earlier Stephen had stood for the same reason.

"My brothers," he began. "I have lived all my life with a perfectly clean conscience before God. I —"

Suddenly the high priest barked an order, and an attendant punched Paul in the mouth. Paul staggered back a step, his lip bleeding.

"God will strike you, you whitewashed wall!" he shouted. "You sit there to judge me according to the law. Yet you break the law by ordering him to strike me!"

"You insult God's high priest!" snapped the attendant.

"My brothers," said Paul. "I did not know he was the high priest. It is written, 'You must not speak evil of the rulers of your people.' "

An attendant punching Paul

An angry murmur arose among the members of the council. Paul knew that among them were many of the party of Sadducees. This sect did not believe in the resurrection of the dead at the last day or in angels or spirits. But the Pharisees believed in all these things. So Paul made a brilliant move.

"Brothers!" he shouted. "I am a Pharisee. Is it for our hope in the resurrection of the dead that I am on trial just now?"

At this the council erupted. A fierce argument broke out between Sadducees and Pharisees. Some of the Pharisees shouted, "We find nothing wrong in this man. Suppose a spirit or an angel has spoken to him!"

The Sadducees rushed at Paul. The Pharisees rushed at the Sadducees. Again Lysias had to

"I am a Pharisee"

step in.

His soldiers whisked Paul out of the hall and back to the palace tower.

That night, in a cell high in the tower, Paul knelt at his bed and prayed. Suddenly the room became light as day. There, just as he had appeared on the road to Damascus, Jesus came to him.

"Courage," Jesus said. "You have spoken of me here in Jerusalem, and you must do the same in Rome."

Just then, in another part of the palace, a centurion knocked at the door to the commander's quarters. "Commander," he said, bowing, "a young man has just come to me with some urgent news for you."

"Send him in at once," said Lysias.

Jesus speaking to Paul

A PRISONER

The man entered. "I am the nephew of your prisoner, Paul," he said. "In the city tonight I overheard some Jews speaking together. They were plotting to kill my uncle. There are over forty of them. They have vowed not to eat or drink anything until they have murdered him."

Lysias put his hand on the man's shoulder. "Thank you for telling me this," he said. "Do not tell anyone that you have come here."

Turning to the centurion Lysias commanded, "Bring the prisoner!"

That night, under a moonless sky, two hundred foot soldiers marched out of the palace, with seventy horsemen and two hundred spearmen. In their midst, wrapped in a heavy cloak and hood, rode Paul.

Through the night they traveled north and late

Sharing about a murder plot

the next day reached Caesarea. They came to the palace of Felix, the governor.

"Greetings in the name of Claudius Lysias," said the commander of the troops. "We bring you a prisoner, whom some Jews in Jerusalem have sworn to kill. Claudius wishes this prisoner to be here under your protection."

The governor gave orders for Paul to be kept in his own headquarters. Five days later the high priest bustled into the palace followed by several priests and a lawyer named Tertullus. The high priest came before Felix and asked that Paul be tried before them all. When the governor had called Paul in, he told the priests to state their case against him.

"Your excellency!" began Tertullus, bowing. "Your wise leadership has brought us a long

"Your excellency!"

period of peace. We welcome this everywhere and at all times, and we are deeply grateful to you. I beg you to be kind and listen to our brief account.

"We found this man to be a dangerous nuisance. He starts riots among the Jews all over the world and is a leader of the party of Nazarenes. He also tried to defile the temple, so we arrested him. If you question him yourself, you will find these accusations true."

Felix now motioned to Paul.

"Your honor," Paul began, "twelve days ago I went to Jerusalem to worship. The Jews did not find me stirring up trouble anywhere. Nor can they prove any of the accusations they bring against me. I do admit this to you, that I worship the God of our ancestors by following that Way

Defending himself to Felix

which they say is false. But I also believe everything written in the law of Moses and the books of the prophets. I have the same hope in God that these themselves have, that people will rise from death.

"While I was in the temple for the ritual of purification, some Jews from Asia saw me and caused an uproar. They themselves ought to be here now to accuse me before you, if they have anything against me. Or let these men here explain what crime *they* found me guilty of."

Felix stood up. "You may go," he said to the priests. To Paul he said, "I will decide your case when Lysias arrives. Meanwhile, you will remain here under guard, but you have the freedom to go about the palace and to have your friends visit you, if you like."

On Trial

A PRISONER

But Felix did not decide Paul's case. Instead he kept him a prisoner and called for him often to hear him speak about Jesus. Something about Paul's message made Felix want to hear it again and again.

Two years later, in July of 59 A.D., Felix was called back to Rome. A new governor, Porcius Festus, was sent to Caesarea in Felix's place.

Still Paul remained a prisoner.

On hearing that a new governor was in Caesarea, the priests in Jerusalem came to bring charges against Paul again. After two years of pent-up hatred and frustration, they now shouted and fumed. They could not even state a clear case.

Finally Festus motioned them to silence and let Paul respond.

Two years in Prison

Paul simply said, "I have done nothing wrong against the law of the Jews or against the temple or against the Roman Empire."

Festus stirred in his seat. He knew Paul was not guilty of any crime. But as the new governor here, he wished to find favor with the Jews. So he asked Paul, "Are you willing to go to Jerusalem and be tried on these charges before me there?"

"I am standing before the emperor's own judgment court, where I should be tried," said Paul. "I have done no wrong to the Jews, as you well know. If I have done something that deserves the death penalty, I do not ask to escape it. But if there is no truth in the charges they bring against me, no one can hand me over to them. I appeal to the emperor."

I appeal to the Emperor

A PRISONER

A Roman citizen's appeal to the emperor had to be granted, if the case was important enough. First Festus whispered among his advisors. Then he said, "You have appealed to the emperor. To the emperor you shall go."

Paul made this appeal not because he was afraid of the Jews, but because Jesus had said, "You must speak of me in Rome." Paul knew he must go to Rome.

"To the Emperor you shall go"

Paul on board ship

8
To Rome

Paul started for Rome in a single-masted coastal vessel, small and light. The Roman centurion in charge was called Julius, and he commanded a dozen soldiers. Bound for the north, the ship carried light cargo and several prisoners, who were chained to timbers below deck. Because he was a Roman citizen who had not been convicted of a crime, Paul was allowed to go free on the ship. With him had come Luke and Aristarchus, who were listed on the ship's roster as Paul's personal servants. To show his prisoner status, Paul wore a light chain on his wrist.

They set sail in the last week of August, 59

A.D., and traveled north from Caesarea, along the coast. The first day they made sixty-seven miles and put in at the port of Sidon.

Julius admired Paul. From the first day out, the centurion could clearly see that Paul was no ordinary prisoner. He was not tall or broad, yet he had the wiry, gnarled look of a man used to hardships and outdoor travel. His beard was gray now and flecked with white. Out of his lined and weathered, lean and hard-edged face, Paul's gaze showed a fierce intelligence, a mind honed sharper and sharper by the passing years. Never before had Julius seen the depth and power that appeared in Paul's eyes. There was nothing weak or false about this man, Julius knew.

From Sidon they continued north and west, heading for the island of Cyprus. A westerly

Julius admired Paul

breeze blew up, the wind of late summer on the Mediterranean. This meant the ship could not sail south of Cyprus and out into the open sea. Instead it had to round the northern tip of the island and travel along the northern coast, where the wind was calmer.

Just north of Cyprus lay the Cilician mainland. The ship moved in closer to this shore and sailed in the shadow of the Taurus Mountains that rose up along the shore.

But the going was slow. The late-summer sun beat down, only rarely did a breeze dance across the sea. It was mid-September when they finally put in at the harbor of Myra.

Here Paul saw several naval galleys, their long oars resting in the water, as they lay at anchor. A few massive merchant ships, carrying wheat and

Sailing the Mediterranean

corn from the East, floated nearby. Myra was a key port in late summer, when the ocean winds made the long voyage to Rome dangerous. Many ships wintered here.

The season was now late, but there were yet many sailing days. Everyone aboard Paul's ship disembarked for another, larger vessel, a merchant ship bound for Rome. Many passengers crowded aboard — merchants, army veterans, university students, and women and children. Including Paul's party, there would be two hundred and eighty people.

This ship, too, had only one mast with a huge mainsail. The danger of this was that the high winds of the open sea could strain that large mast to the point of cracking support timbers. Julius and his soldiers prayed to their Roman gods for

Loading into a Merchant ship

fair weather. Of all the people aboard, only Paul and his friends were at peace.

On the sixteenth day of September they set sail. The intended course was just south of the island of Rhodes in the archipelagoes, then due west and around the southern tip of Greece before heading north by the strait of Messina. This was the safest, most direct course to Rome.

But the weather chose another course. A strong northwester soon blew up. It was impossible to sail into such a wind, so the ship's captain again hugged the southern Cilician shore. They came this way to the port of Cnidus at the tip of a long, mountainous peninsula jutting out into the sea.

Here was the farthest point they could reach still protected by land against the northwester.

Map of journey

Now the captain had to sail south and west for the large island of Crete, hoping the wind would turn soon.

They reached the island after several days. Here they rounded the eastern cape of Salmone and struggled along the southern coast of Crete for yet many more days. They stopped at a little town called Fair Havens. Perhaps here they could wait out the wind.

But it was now mid-October. By the second week of November all sea travel would cease for the winter. The winter sky would be overcast, making navigation by the stars impossible. Time was running out.

Fair Havens was a bad place to winter. It was exposed to the sea on three sides. In the violent winter storms a ship at anchor here could be

Fair Havens

driven aground on the jagged rocks. No lodging was available in the tiny village. All the passengers would have to stay aboard through the winter. The captain urged an attempt to sail along the southern coast of this island to the port of Phoenix. There, he said, was a safe harbor and winter lodging. By now Julius had learned of Paul's seafaring experience. He asked his advice.

"I can see, gentlemen," said Paul, "that this voyage will be disastrous. It will mean grave loss, not only of ship and cargo, but also of life." Julius did not know what to think.

Then the wind changed. It came in from the south, gentle and steady. Julius decided to ignore Paul's warning. They set sail.

The sea was calm, the sky clear. The gentle southern breeze filled the mainsail, and the ship

"This voyage will be disatrous"

sailed smoothly across the gulf toward Phoenix.

But again the wind changed. It came howling down from Mount Ida and across the gulf with an evil fury. Thick, black clouds blotted out the sun. Suddenly the sea became covered with whitecaps and seethed. The captain came to Julius and Paul. His face was pale.

"The Levanter is upon us!" he cried. "The northeaster. It hits at this time of year, though it is early. I thought we would outrun it."

"What will happen to us?" shouted Julius over the roar of the wind.

"We cannot sail against this!" cried the captain. "Our only hope is to give way and run before it."

"But it will drive us straight out to sea!"

We cannot sail against this

"We have no choice!"

Now the worst happened. The violent wind cracked the support timbers. Seawater seeped into the hull.

In the force of that gale, the ship scudded over the sea, plunging and rising with the waves. Every able-bodied man aboard took turns at the pumps. But the sea came in faster than they could pump it out. The ship squatted lower and lower into the water. Cargo and tackle were pitched overboard to lighten the load.

Fourteen days passed like this.

The rain drove down in sheets, the wind raged, the waves rolled. Julius and the crew sat huddled on deck, drenched, hopeless, waiting for death. Paul came up to them.

"You should have listened to me," he said.

The sea raging

"But now, I beg you, take courage! Last night an angel stood by me and said, 'Do not be afraid, Paul. You must stand before the emperor. And God has given you the lives of all who sail with you.' So, take heart, men. I believe God will do just as he promised.

"Now come," continued Paul. He picked up a loaf of bread. "We have not eaten in fourteen days. Eat now, to regain strength. Believe me, not one of you will be lost." Paul gave thanks to God and ate.

At this the crew began stirring. Their faces brightened. They, too, took bread and began to eat.

Just before dawn the next day the ship suddenly lurched. "We have struck sand!" cried the captain. "It must be an island. Everyone will

Giving thanks to God

have to abandon ship, before we are smashed to
pieces in the waves. Hurry!"

It was almost too late. The ship began breaking up. Some swam, some held onto pieces of
timber and wreckage, but everyone made it to
shore. They had landed on the tiny island of
Malta. Together the sodden, starving passengers
and crew tramped ashore in the drenching rain.

The natives had seen the ship and rushed down
to the beach and lit a large fire to warm the sur-
vivors. Some had brought food. Paul helped
gather firewood. As he carried a bundle of sticks,
a poisonous snake suddenly shot out of the bundle and latched onto his hand. When they saw it,
the natives drew back from him. They believed
their gods must be punishing Paul for some
wicked crime. The bite of that snake was deadly.

Snake bit!

Carefully they watched, expecting Paul to drop dead.

The apostle simply shook the snake off into the roaring fire and went about his work. When it was clear he was not going to die, the natives began talking excitedly among themselves. "He must be a god!" they said.

So they brought Paul to the estate of the chief magistrate of the island, Publius. The magistrate's father lay sick in bed, so delirious with a fever he could not see or speak.

Paul walked up to the man's bed. He took him by the hand and said, "In the name of the Lord Jesus Christ, get up!"

The natives gasped. The magistrate's father opened his eyes and sat up. A healthy flush rose

Healing the magistrate's father

to his cheeks. He climbed out of bed, wonder in his face.

"Jesus Christ has made you well," said Paul. That day many sick people came to Paul, and he laid hands on them. All were healed.

The travelers stayed there through the winter. Many natives and many of the crew and passengers became believers in Christ as Paul taught and preached.

In the spring they sailed again, going north past Sicily and on up the western coast of Italy to the port of Puteoli.

From here they set out on foot on the great paved Roman highway, the Appian Way. As they crossed the last shoulder of the Alban hills, Rome lay before them.

On the Roman highway

With a million citizens and more than a million slaves, Rome was the greatest city Paul had ever seen. But the sight of this place did not awe him.

Paul carried no sword. No army followed. The chain of a prisoner hung from his wrist. Yet he came to Rome that day not as prisoner, but as conqueror.

He did not know what lay ahead.

He could not know that hundreds of people in Rome would become Christians because of his testimony there.

He would never know that in only a few years the worst persecution in all of history would fall on Christians in Rome, under the reign of the evil Nero.

To escape, the Christians would retreat into

Paul in Rome

the catacombs, the vast labyrinth under the streets of Rome. There, in the darkness of those caverns and tunnels, the believers' faith would burn like a thousand torches. When they emerged again, they would conquer Rome and the world for Christ.

Paul could not know that the Christian faith would remain strong in the cities where he had preached, or that it would grow and spread throughout the world.

Millions upon millions of lives would be changed, over more than nineteen centuries, because of a handful of letters he had written to young Christian churches still under his care.

Paul did not know these things as he tramped down the street into Rome. He was just a servant. His master had spoken, and he had obeyed.

This was his last mission.

The Apostel Paul

 **Books for Kids!**

Young Reader's Christian Library
Action, Adventure, and Fun Reading!

This series for young readers ages 8 to 15 is action-packed, fast-paced, and Christ-centered! With exciting illustrations on every other page following the text, kids won't be able to put these books down! Over 100 illustrations per book. All books are paperbound.

The unique size (4-3/16" X 5-3/8") makes these books easy to take anywhere!

A Selection to Satisfy All Kids!

At the Back of the North Wind
Ben-Hur
Corrie ten Boom
David Livingstone
Dark Secrets of the Ouija, The
Elijah
Hudson Taylor
In His Steps
Jesus

Joseph
Miriam
Paul
Pilgrim's Progress, The
Robinson Crusoe
Ruth
Swiss Family Robinson, The
Thunder in the Valley

Available at Christian Book Stores Everywhere.
or order from:
Barbour and Company, Inc.
P.O. Box 719
Uhrichsville, Ohio 44683

$2.50 each retail, plus $1.00 for postage and handling per order.
Prices subject to change without notice.